the de
han

the delhi walla
hangouts

mayank austen soofi

designed by solveig marina bang

Collins

First published in India in 2010 by Collins
An imprint of HarperCollins *Publishers*
a joint venture with
The India Today Group

ISBN: 978-93-5029-006-4

2 4 6 8 10 9 7 5 3 1

HarperCollins *Publishers*
A-53, Sector 57, NOIDA, Uttar Pradesh – 201301, India
77-85 Fulham Palace Road, London W6 8JB, United Kingdom
Hazelton Lanes, 55 Avenue Road, Suite 2900, Toronto,
Ontario M5R 3L2 and 1995 Markham Road, Scarborough,
Ontario M1B 5M8, Canada
25 Ryde Road, Pymble, Sydney, NSW 2073, Australia
31 View Road, Glenfield, Auckland 10, New Zealand
10 East 53rd Street, New York NY 10022, USA

Project Editor: Sheema Mookherjee
Typeset in Calisto MT 8/12

Printed and bound at
Gopsons Papers Ltd.

Contents

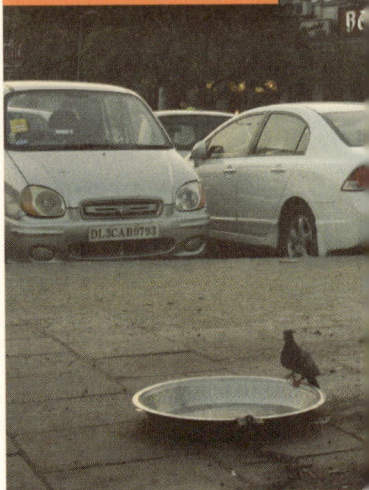

Shop

Connaught Place

Khan Market

Dilli Haat

Sarojini Nagar Market

Select Citywalk

Basant Lok Market

Karol Bagh

Shahpur Jat

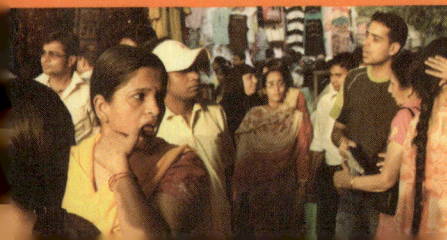

Beautiful, circular and walker-friendly, the British-built Connaught Place (CP), now renamed Rajiv Chowk, has a kaleidoscopic character.

It is at various times serene (early morning), business-like (noon), romantic (evening)

and mischievous (night). The high-vaulted, pillared corridors of the Inner Circle and Outer Circle are lined with shops, restaurants and offices.

Over the years individually-owned landmark shops have given way to retail chain showrooms and fast-food outlets. Single-screen theatres have been renovated into multiplexes. Bookshops have relocated, photo studios have rolled down their shutters, and laidback restaurants, steeped in nostalgia, have become history.

shop

Take the metro to Rajiv Chowk and come up in **Central Park**. Once home to Delhi's low life, it is now as sanitized as any middle-class hangout can get. In the evenings, couples lounge on the grass and families sit around chatting in circles.

Walk into **Palika Bazaar**, Delhi's first underground air-conditioned market. Known for pirated DVDs and fake branded wear, it's a great place for picking up bargains on bags, footwear and clothing. The park above is like what the 'old' Central Park used to be. Hemmed in by the CP skyline, lovers neck, ear-cleaners look for custom, eunuchs beg for money and lonely gays cruise for emergency love.

Stroll leisurely through CP's **Inner Circle**. Lined with showrooms and restaurants, the pavement is crowded with 20-somethings plugged into iPods, shoppers snacking on bhelpuri, office-goers gossiping during smoking breaks, Gujarati women hawking embroidered textiles in American-accented English, and flute sellers playing tunes. Try chicken stroganoff at the old-world **Embassy Restaurant** (D-11). See the latest bestsellers at **The New Book Depot** (B-18) run by an eccentric but adorable man, whose father bought the store from a French couple.

To enjoy some Bollywood masala get a cinema ticket to **The Regal**, New Delhi's first cinema hall, circa 1932. It hosted the Indian premiere of *Gone with the Wind* in 1940 and was frequented by Prime Minister Nehru. Today, its grand staircase and historical past compensates for its rundown look. At 1 Regal Building find the legendary piano shop, **A. Godin & Co**, its windows decked with sitars. Harmoniums lie on tables and guitars adorn

the walls, but the teak pianos create the atmosphere, their old-world splendour suffusing the shop with a charm that is becoming rare in CP.

Spruce up your wardrobe at **Janpath Flea Market** across from The Regal. Scout around for colourful tees, skirts, kurtis, harem pants and accessories. A second-hand bookshop there stocks occasional wonders.

A late evening walk around CP's **Outer Circle** gives you glimpses of its inner life. Attendants handle the day's last customers. In cafés, solitary souls have their suppers. At the bus stops, day-jobbers wait impatiently with their lunch boxes and briefcases. Outside the metro station, tormented lovers count the minutes to the farewell hour. Doped beggars huddle together on pavements to smoke hashish while street children peddle balloons. The dimly-lit **@Live bar** (K-12) strikes the right mood with live music, as does **Blues** (N-19), a favourite rock music joint.

For the best view of the **CP Skyline**, walk to New Delhi railway station and climb the footbridge. The scene is not exactly Manhattan-like but it makes a Delhiite's heart swell with pride.

9

shop

If Delhi were New York City, Khan Market would be its Upper East Side. A freshly-botoxed woman steps out of the up-scale skin clinic in her Jimmy Choo heels. A young man in a faded blue Ed Hardy T-shirt asks for the latest *New Yorker* at a foreign magazines' stall. A pot-bellied man, his spindly, hairy legs slanting out of his red Puma shorts, talks into his iPhone outside the florist selling exotic lilies and orchids. Rows of Volkswagens, BMWs and Pajeros honk for parking space outside—the only free thing in this market patronized by the expats and elite of the city.

People in Khan Market live the dream. Inflation is just

a headline in the *International Herald Tribune*.

Suddenly there is a ripple in the crowd. An important person has been spotted. Whispers spread from **Good Earth** home décor store to **Chonas** restaurant in the front lane, up to **Big Chill** on the first floor and down again to **Mamagoto** in the lane below. Is it Sonia Gandhi? No, it's the Prime Minister's wife! Heads crane towards a cluster of Black Cat commandos. With an air of polite reserve, the first lady walks into **Dayal Opticals**. People nod their heads in confirmation and carry on. A silver-haired lady in a white sari walks off, holding a **Fabindia** paper bag, a style statement in itself.

shop

MAGAZINES
PULL
Pull
VISA

EL PAIS
FORCE
Civil Society
Biblio:

Inside the landmark **Bahrisons Booksellers** (far left) a middle-aged man asks for a book called *How to Please Your Wife*. A part-time politician and Page 3 personality is sitting on a low stool and thinking to herself, 'This book, that book, and that book too.' A well-known author is complaining to the shop assistant, 'Why is my book not on the window display?'

A young college student flips through the latest Paulo Coelho, places it back on the shelf and exits. She walks past the magazine stall and doggie shops, past **Blanco** restaurant into **Choko La**—no empty table. She comes out, wonders whether she will eat a kathi roll standing on the road, like most of her peers.

She changes her mind, walks to the other side, enters **Full Circle** bookshop, and climbs up to **Café Turtle**. The pasta of the day is fusilli served with a rich arrabiata sauce. Her Khan Market excursion will end with this meal.

Dilli Haat
Village market

Where Yusuf Sarai
Open 10am-10pm (7 days)

In a city as disconnected from rural craftspeople as Delhi, it is refreshing to enter Dilli Haat, the food and crafts bazaar spread over six acres and modelled to look like a north Indian village. The entrance plaque has the image of two belles churning milk into butter. Inside, the paved walks, brick stalls with thatched roofs, the occasional sarangi players and the open sky above give one the temporary illusion of being in a haat or village market. The dream may sometimes be broken by the loud bargaining of Delhi shoppers, but the colourful products of the artisans, who arrive from far to display their wares, is a great opportunity to shop for all your ethnic presents and souvenirs at one stop.

Take a walk down the chief passageways along both sides of the courtyard, which are lined with **stalls selling colourful handicrafts** from different regions. No matter how much you may be tempted by Kullu shawls, Rajasthani cholis, Punjabi jootis, Lucknawi chikankari kurtas, Kolhapuri chappals, bead necklaces, metal pendants, glass bangles, brass statues or wicker chairs, do a recce before you buy—the next handloom textiles, Northeast handicrafts, Dastakar Mela, Delhi Utsav, and many more.

Another crowd puller are the **food stalls**, each specialising in the typical cuisine of India's many states. The cooking is so authentic and the prices so moderate that there is no better way to savour a sumptuous Pan-Indian banquet. Try the wazwan meal at the Kashmir stall. Their gostaba, rista and dum aloo is delicious; so is the saffron kehva on a winter's day. The Maharashtra stall is probably the only place in Delhi where you get zunka bhakar and thali pith. For the very adventurous, nothing is more daring than the fried pork ribs and curries at the Nagaland stall, which are laced with raja mirchi, the world's hottest chilli. The best momos are found at the Manipur stall, although Sikkim and Meghalaya are not far behind.

Outside, **unofficial stalls** attract an equal number of clients. Women get their hands decorated with henna and girls get their hair braided with coloured threads. Chaiwallas go round with kettles, ice cream carts are stationed on the boundary and the candyfloss man rings his bell.

stall always seems to have a better selection and prices!

See the Madhubani paintings and papier-mâché curios from Bihar. Equally fascinating are the pointillist animal paintings by artists from Bastar and metal dhokra sculpture. Prices of folk art range from Rs 150 to Rs 30,000.

Dilli Haat organizes **theme-based festivals** every month. Look out for the banner over the gate and you will see announcements of festivals for organic food,

shop

Think of Sarojini Nagar market, or SN, as the setting of a trashy fairy tale. It is fit for a beautiful princess robbed of her kingdom and left with little to buy a dress for the evening ball where she is to meet her dream prince. A haven for bargains, SN is the people's bazaar. On sale—T-shirts, skirts, frocks, jeans, sandals, saris, lehengas, nighties, hankies, bags, inflatable bathtubs, hair pins, toys, pillows, suitcases, plastic tulips, Italian softy and bunta, among other things unimaginable.

Every serious shopper converges here—from students on a budget to bored housewives, tourists from other states, and East Europeans. Fronting the larger shops and showrooms are hundreds of makeshift stalls—all lined with a colourful melee. Leather bags hang from tree branches, lurid pink bras wave in the breeze, T-shirts lie in untidy mounds, and cheap mannequins wearing halters startle you out of nowhere. You can pick up T-shirts at Rs 50, dresses at Rs 200 and tops at Rs 100—fashionable largesse from the world of export rejects. You can even hunt for fake labels and walk away with Gap, Tommy Hilfiger and Lacoste—who's to know anyway?

Sarojini Nagar Market
Everything and more

Where South Delhi
Open 11am-8pm
(closed Mon)

An anthropologist could write a book by sitting at the bazaar entrance and observing life. Old women sell lemons and guavas, middle-class matrons rest on benches, migrant workers dig up cable lines, caste-crossed lovers meet under the peepal trees, sunken-cheeked boys hawk handkerchiefs, showroom security guards grumble on cell phones, beggars drag themselves across the pavement, unemployed youth play carrom, and chauffeur-driven women bargain over Rs 10.

SN is a kind of mad-fun place, where, laden with your bags of shopping, you can stop for Punjabi chhole bhature, followed by Tibetan momos and Bengali rasgulla. If you are the type that believes life was better 100 years ago, think again. Then there was no SN.

shop

Select Citywalk
Mall heaven

Where Saket
Open 10am-10pm (7 days)

Happiness is no longer an elusive abstraction. It can be seen, chased, examined, occasionally bargained for, and purchased at Select Citywalk, Saket. Opposite Khirki village, the mall's gleaming glass and neon facade is the gateway to Delhi's happy materialism. Within its 1.3 million sq ft, Delhiites experience life of the first world.

They buy jeans from Zara, tote bags from Mango and linen shirts from Promod. They indulge in Häagen-Dazs ice creams and Patchi chocolates. They order latte at Barista and Greek salad (loaded with feta cheese) at Coffee Bean and Tea Leaves. The outdoor plaza, hosting art exhibitions and music concerts, serves as an escape for the shopping weary.

You do not have to be a mall rat to be bedazzled by Select Citywalk. Sample the stats: three floors, 19 elevators, 21 escalators, 21 eating joints and 140 apparel stores. Maximum parking capacity is 2,000 cars, which is sometimes not enough on weekends. On dull weekdays, the daily footfall is 20,000. On Wednesday's flea market, it rises to 35,000. On weekends, it's 50,000. The maximum capacity, before security shuts the gates, is 125,000.

In the Christmas season, Select Citywalk installs Delhi's biggest Christmas tree.

shop

Basant Lok Market
Happening hub

Where Vasant Vihar
Open 10am-8pm
(closed Tue)

In the heart of posh Vasant Vihar, this bustling shopping centre has a history. India's first McDonald's opened here in 1996, as did the first TGIF (now closed). The legendary Priya was one of the few cinemas to screen English movies in the old days, and is now the flagship property of **PVR Cinemas**, India's first multiplex chain. One of Delhi's most eclectic bookstores, **Fact & Fiction** (above), is situated here. When vodka was first served in a golgappa, it also happened here, at **Punjabi by Nature** restaurant.

Homesick Westerners have freshly-baked croissants and steaming hot coffee at **Choko La** (top right), and pick up cheeses, smoked salmon and sliced turkey at **Modern Bazaar**, the well-

stocked supermarket that has every exotic ingredient under the sun. For desi delights like kebabs and dal makhani, there is always **Nirula's**, again one of the oldest outlets of this iconic chain in the city.

At night the market buzzes with people out to have a good time—movies, pubbing, eating out and partying. Although the discothèque **RPM** is a bit noisy and juvenile because of its large school student clientele, **Turquoise Cottage**, Delhi's first rock music hub, is a perfect zone for those who swear by Lennon, Bono and all alternative rock music artists. While its sheen has paled a bit by the coming of the malls, Basant Lok retains its importance as a great place to ogle at the city's beautiful people.

shop

If the only reason to visit Chandni Chowk is to feed on chaat and laddu, then the only rationale for being in Karol Bagh is to buy saris and sehras. However, these are just the several clichés about Delhi. Karol Bagh is a residential and commercial district in west-central Delhi. Once home to mainly Muslims, most of whom left for Pakistan after the Partition, it metamorphosed with the arrival of Hindu refugees from Pakistani Punjab.

Today the area is popular as a shopping destination for bourgeois Delhi. In 2006, Manju Kapur set her novel *Home*, about an unhappy middle-class family, in this neighbourhood. (Guess how the family made its living? It ran a sari showroom.) However, Kapur's suffocating Karol Bagh is misleading. The place has energy and exudes warmth. Giant hoardings turn the skyline into a multi-coloured fantasy, mannequins seem as alive as the sales assistants, and people shop as if recession was yesterday's headline.

On Ajmal Khan Road, the area's premier shopping district, the flea stalls (handbags on tree branches, chappals on car bonnets) coexist harmoniously with their big-brand neighbours.

Karol Bagh
Saris and much more

Where Central Delhi
Open 11am-8pm
(closed Mon)

Apart from the mega jewellery and sari stores, there are old time favourites such as Roopak for spices, Impressions for nail varnish and eyeliners, and Sirs & Hers for all the branded garments. Across the road, is the Ghaffar Market, famous for its smuggled iPods and iPhones. The streets here are also lined with shops selling pretty buttons, laces and imported clips, making it a virtual Barbie-land.

The bazaar is also a haven for food lovers—Anjalika's pastry and sandwiches, Roshan's kulfis, Sardar ki tikkis, pavement popcorns, and the roasted shakarkandi and fruit stalls. Towards Jhandewalan, the evening comes alive with makeshift street food stalls selling a vast variety of kebabs, fried snacks (fish fry by the kilo and anda pakoda are famous) sweetmeats, and more.

JAI MATA DI
FANCY LADIES TOP
TOP
LUDHIANA ~~175~~
HOSIERY
COTTON 150
Rs
No BARGAINING

Reetone
Reebok

EASYTONE
BETTER LEGS AND BETTER BUTT WITH EVERY STEP

Westend
Tailors
Reebok
MOHAN LAL & SO
BOOKSELLERS & STATIONERS

shop

Shahpur Jat
Fashion village

Where South Delhi
Open 11am-8pm

The urban village of Shahpur Jat is artsy, boisterous, cosmopolitan, chaotic, dusty, historical, and pulses with energy close to its rural soul. Elders smoke hookahs in the squares, strains of film music waft from apartment windows and SUVs rumble through the outer lanes. More than 100 fashion boutiques are clustered on the village's periphery. Inside, the streets are lined with tailoring sweatshops employing kaarigars (craftsmen). Local women rarely come out without purdah, while the designer women strut around in stilettos, making rounds between their showrooms and 'units'. Artists, students and young professionals who live in Shahpur Jat give it a bohemian flavour.

In 1303, Alauddin Khilji founded the first Muslim city of Delhi, Siri, in Shahpur Jat.

Nothing remains of it, except parts of its wall, a mosque and a structure called baradari. Shahpur Jat's modern history began 900 years ago when its farmlands spread from Hauz Khas and Andrewsganj to Greater Kailash and Malviya Nagar. In 1978, the government acquired the lands on which were raised the posh colonies of Asiad Village, Panchsheel Park and Hauz Khas. While the village emerged as a centre for basement workshops and its migrant population bloated, the ex-farmers discovered gold in real estate. The big fortune came with the arrival of boutiques at the turn of the century.

Rutty and pockmarked, Jangi House lane is Shahpur Jat's high couture street lined with high-end, as well as affordable fashion labels. The customer base is serious and loyal. Priyanka Gandhi has been spotted here. Maya (5I), like most boutiques in the area, deals in wedding trousseaus, customized outfits, and informal wear such as kurtas and tunics.

shop

A lilac-coloured formal tube dress costs Rs 2,500. Maximum store (5J/1) rents out space to art exhibitions (Rs 5,000 for 10 days). Home Linen (5K/1) has introduced Pakistani cotton suits (ranging from Rs 1,000).

Take a break from shopping at Cheenos (86B, above). Started in 2008 as a tattoo parlour, it offers coffee, juices and hookah smoking. Dimly lit and attended by a young cheery staff, it offers respite from the pseudo-rustic world outside. The tattoo artist is available by appointment.

At The Shoe Garage House (118B), the peep toes, pumps, strappy sandals, boots and wedges are of leather and suede; stylish, smart and affordable. It attracts a large student crowd. There is a café nearby, as well as a Slice of Italy outlet. Book lovers may go to Bookwise book studio (125A), and the arty types may hang out at the Reflection Art gallery (40A).

The left lane, off the front of Nigam Pratibha Vidyapeeth, a primary school for girls, skirts a Siri-era stonewall. At the other end lies the plain-looking Tohfa Wali Gumbad. An early 14th-century ruin, it is rarely seen by anyone except some of the fashion boutique kaarigars whose windows look on to it.

Hauz Khas Village
Emerging chique

Where Off Hauz Khas
Open 11am-8pm
(closed Mon)

Stroll

Hauz Khas Village

Majnu ka Tila

Paharganj

Matia Mahal

Chandni Chowk

In its heyday Hauz Khas village was described by *The New York Times* as the 'national capital of ethnic chic.' Nobody imagined that this rustic outpost overshadowed by scenic 14th-century ruins could be transformed into a shopping destination. In 1988, Bina Ramani, Delhi's original society queen and the first Indian designer to be featured on the cover of *Vogue*, set up a boutique here.

Its success led to more boutiques, followed by art galleries, antique reproduction showrooms, bookshops, cafes and night clubs. Today, shops and restaurants have relocated, and there are other ethnic shopping hubs in the city. Yet the village remains a nostalgic hangout.

The **Kunzum Travel Café** (above) is run on a 'pay what you like' basis for its offerings of coffee, tea and cookies. Aimed at the itinerant soul, the bookrack has *Lonely Planet* guides and travel magazines. Visitors pin paper chits on a board announcing their next destination, and the walls are full of travel photographs. Besides free wi-fi, you are welcome to plug your iPod into the music system. The window looks onto a temple, and you may sit here all day without being made to feel uncomfortable. The venue hosts jam sessions and poetry readings. In a city where most cafes justify the high cost of their mediocre cappuccinos by offering air-conditioned pretentiousness, Kunzum is a relief.

Nearby, the **Cottage of Arts & Jewels** is a basement shop cluttered with old books, Hindi film posters, dusty chandeliers, camel-bone pendants, faded maps and vintage clothes said to have come down from the wardrobes of royal families.

The **Indian Art Bazaar** offers kitschy furniture of the past, such as almirahs, and even complete doorways, perhaps harvested from old havelis. Hauz Khas has many stores dealing in antique reproductions. One has a brass replica of the world's first globe priced at Rs 9,950 and elephant-headed walking sticks at Rs 1,000.

The **Prabhu** bookshop has its shelves stuffed with pricey, antique books on history, mountaineering and wildlife, some dating from the 19th century. The store also has Raj-era photographs ranging between Rs 500 and 4,000.

The **Gung Korean Royal Gallery** (above left) is perhaps the only place in Delhi selling Korean artifacts such as paper lamps, wooden chests, mirrors and ethnic dolls. The owner is Korean and shuttles between Delhi and Seoul.

Dimly-lit **Yodakin** (top) bookstore, run by an independent publisher of the same name, displays coffee table volumes and paperbacks, which are critically acclaimed but not popular enough to be stocked in regular bookshops. Also on sale are DVDs by filmmakers such as Kurosawa, Ray, Bergman and Truffaut. The shop is very welcoming to stray dogs, some of which doze by the shelves.

Naivedyam restaurant, offers traditional south Indian snacks and main dishes. The music is Carnatic, the stewards are in mundu and the walls are painted with scenes of Tamil Nadu temple life.

Gunpowder restaurant has no fancy furniture or stylish menu. Yet, it has become quite the rage for authentic non-vegetarian south Indian cuisine. Specializing in dishes such as Andhra mutton, toddy shop fish curry, and Coorgi pork, it has acquired a cult following. The terrace looks onto the lake. Facebook or telephone booking is recommended (26535700).

The Living Room Café and Kitchen lounge, aka TLR, has a good bar, eclectic menu, comfy sofas and a languid character. Sipping a cup of coffee on the terrace can be very relaxing. On some weeknights, TLR hosts music gigs.

For rare, old furniture and accessories, go to the **Country Collection** showroom. There are Victorian and Georgian cupboards and writing desks, ethnic charpoys and benches, carved doors, Buddha heads, and reproductions.

Cotton Curio sells women's garments and home furnishings, all in cotton of course, and sourced from Jaipur.

After seeing the ruins, shopping and eating, finish your excursion with a walk in the **Deer Park**, which separates the village from the city. Besides a secluded jogging track, you can see birds, peacocks, rabbits, and, of course, deer.

stroll

Majnu ka Tila
Little Lhasa

Where North Delhi
Open All hours

A Tibetan refugee camp since the 1960s, Majnu ka Tila, or MT in the local lingo, is Delhi's Little Lhasa. Here wrinkled grannies kill time by sitting on pavement benches, chummy uncles drink butter tea, CD shacks play Tibetan pop stars like Phurbu T. Namgyal, and rosy-cheeked boys, fresh from Lhasa, smoke Marlboros on street corners.

Whether it is due to the appeal of the Dalai Lama (smiling from every wall), the pull of Free Tibet romanticism, Buddhist Hollywood star Richard Gere's charisma, or the delicious momos, more and more Delhiites are to be seen hanging out in MT's charming alleyways.

The ambience is mildly spiritual—there are bookshops selling Buddhist prayer books and Tibetan newspapers, and monasteries are filled with incense smoke and Om Mani Padme chants.

Dine at **Dolma House** (House No. 1, No. 10), one of the oldest establishments here. Ask for the steamed momos, although they take their own sweet time to come, since they are cooked only once the order is taken. But why hurry? You'll get the other usual Tibetan suspects here like thukpas and noodles. Try thenthuk, a kind of noodle soup, or the Tibetan sausage. A surprise item at Dolma House is the wonderful strawberry lassi.

Don't look puzzled if the waiter hands you a notebook and a pen along with the menu. In most eateries in MT guests are expected to jot down what they want, to avoid confusion as a result of mispronouncing the names of dishes. Another favourite eatery is Teedees frequented by the St Stephen's crowd. Ask for beef chilli and tongue here, if you are a fan of beef.

The Coffee Shop (seen left, 39th block, New Camp) is a hip establishment situated in a basement. Here modernity mixes seamlessly with Tibetology—saffron-robed lamas tap away on laptops as MT's young-and-cool crowd keeps up with the latest gossip. The coffee is as hearty as in any big retail chain; the brownies are gooey, the fruit cake crumbly. All the baked goods are homemade, and the doughnuts are the most popular among them.

For nirvana, visit the monastery in the principal square at 9am or 6pm, when the monks chant. The prayer room is lit with lamps and the air smells of butter. Don't forget to turn the large prayer wheel at the entrance. Coming out into the square, you'll feel you are in a Tibetan village, but alas, the mountains and yaks will be missing.

stroll

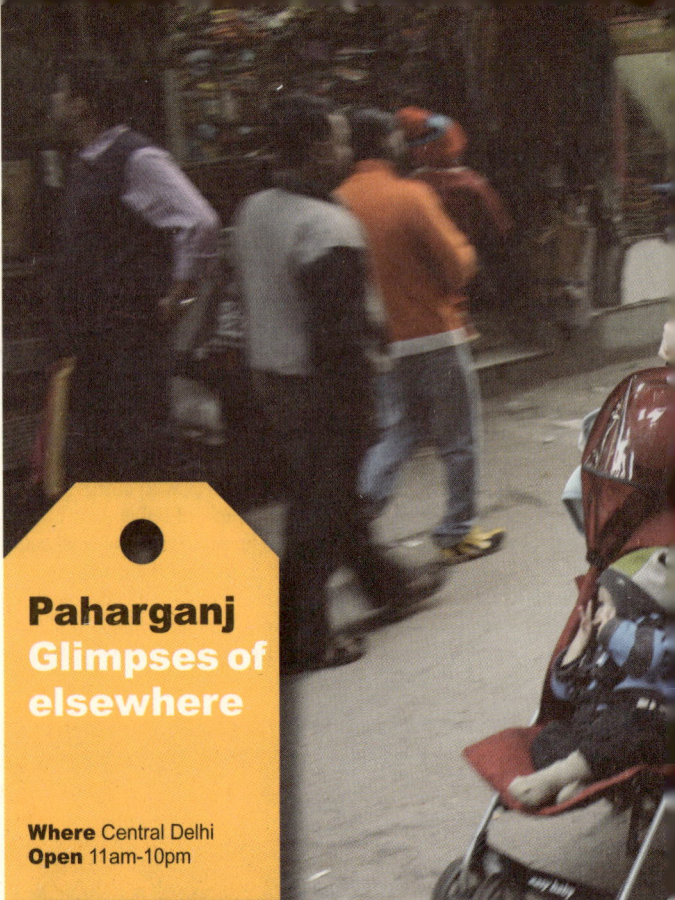

Paharganj
Glimpses of elsewhere

Where Central Delhi
Open 11am-10pm

A haven for Western backpackers, Paharganj encapsulates the essence of white man's India. There are touts, cows, beggars, spice stores, henna parlours, temples, mosques, chai stalls and kebab corners. Plump sari-clad women walk down the bazaar lane, almost rubbing shoulders with half-naked backpackers. The shops, streets and Indians here look like props on a foreign set filled with tourists of different nationalities.

Go to **Appetite** restaurant. Where else in the city can you get yak cheese, avocado

sandwich, palak paneer, chop suey, kimchi rice, ratatouille, lasagne and enchilada under one roof? Paharganj is dotted with such joints, some others being **Sam's** rooftop café and the **German Bakery**.

Try bargaining at the stores selling Bollywood-themed bags, multi-coloured keffiyeh, pendants, rings, jackets, second-hand underwear and even leather whips. This is a wholesale market and the stuff here goes to other bargain bazaars such as Janpath and Sarojini Nagar where, of course, it gets costlier.

stroll

See the shops selling smoking paraphernalia such as chillums, pipes and hookahs—you will bump into numerous boys at shady corners trying to peddle the stuff to put inside.

Go behind the **Imperial Cinema** and turn left to Tilak Gali. This quiet street boasts stunning havelis, old mansions encircling a courtyard. It is like being in the Walled City, but without the crowd.

Browse at **Jackson's** second-hand bookstore. Khan Market may have some of the city's best first-hand bookstores but it is in Paharganj where you get some of the most exciting books, unavailable anywhere else in the city. Partial thanks must go to the visiting backpackers

who sell off their eclectic array of volumes to lighten their loads. Most cafés and bakeries here also stock books.

Have you ever seen a CD shack selling everything from Pink Floyd to Om Mani Padme chants to Allah Hoo, Hare Krishna bhajans, rave music, lounge music and even Dam Maro Dam, Bollywood's greatest hippie song? The nameless store at No 5077 (sometimes known as Bubby's) is one such store, and there are others like it.

Paharganj's jalebis are as juicy as any of those to be had in Chandni Chowk, only a little less sweet and a little less costly. Try some at **Karan's** stall in the main bazaar.

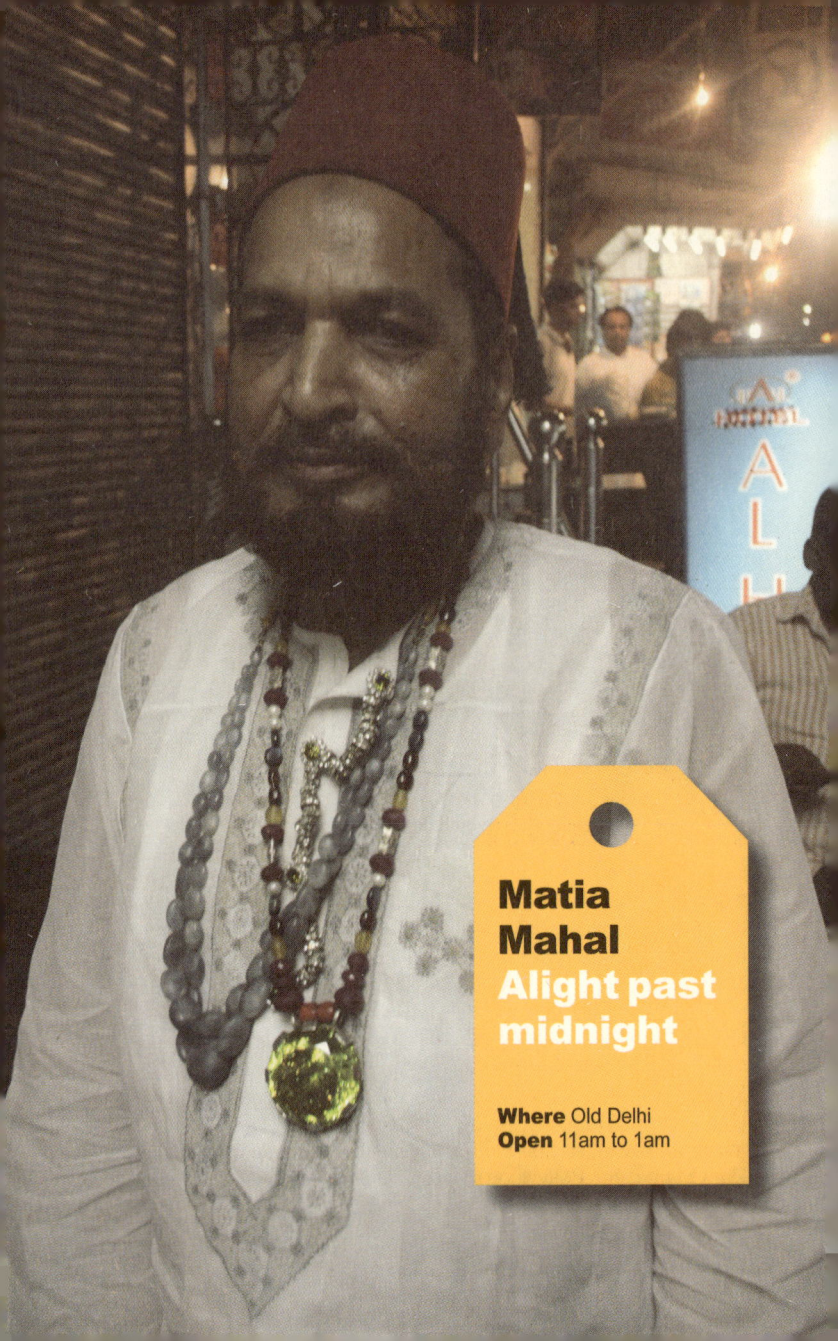

Matia Mahal

Alight past midnight

Where Old Delhi
Open 11am to 1am

The heart of the Walled City, Matia Mahal bazaar, is straight out of the *Arabian Nights*. Here is the land of spicy kebabs, bearded mullahs, veiled women, kaftan-clad beggars, fat goats and cows. Chaotic during the day, it shows its inner life (and beauty) during the late night when the trading instinct weakens and it is time to dine and laugh with friends.

In a city with no shopping area open through the night, Matia Mahal remains lit up past midnight, as if it belongs to a different city with a different code of living. It boasts no malls, nightclub or pubs, yet it's sensuous. Start your exploration at 10pm from Urdu Bazaar, which is lined with bookstores, grubby guesthouses and countless carnivorous eateries selling beef kebabs, keema-kaleji, ishtu and korma. While some of the best bookshops, like **M. Rashid & Sons** and **Maktaba Jamia** (it has an in-house calligrapher who is a treat to watch), have closed for the day, a few stalls remain open where you can browse for Urdu authors not found in the rest of the city.

At this hour, the entire Urdu Bazaar is bathed in an orange neon glow and looks like a scene from a fairy tale. The sights are kaleidoscopic: boys on bikes, kebabs on skewers, chickens in their coops and beggars on trolleys.

Matia Mahal's main alley faces the principal entrance of Jama Masjid, its stone minarets standing like sentinels, watching over the commotion. **Kalan Sweets**, since 1939, is a dessert lover's delight. Among its various offerings is a delicacy called habshi halwah. (Is it because 'habshi' is slang for Africans, and the mithai is black?) Next to it are stalls selling fen, rusks and sewai. All of it comes from bakeries situated deeper in the by-lanes, some of which are still busy stuffing bread into the ovens.

A left lane leads to **Karim's**, Old Delhi's most famous Mughlai restaurant. Not far away, in the main alley, is **Al Sahi Chicken Corner** where juicy birds are being roasted in front of customers. For rice lovers, there are big-bellied vendors selling saffron-flavoured biryani in their huge cauldrons, and the occasional phirniwalla selling this sweet set in earthenware bowls.

The Matia Mahal visit may also be turned into a shopping expedition to acquire Old Delhi

stroll

keepsakes— jootis, pyjamas and costume jewellery. Shops such as **Amaan Garments** and **Fashion Zone** stock readymade garments ranging from Rs 150 to Rs 500. There are beautifully-embroidered burqas too. Bargaining is recommended.

As you walk further into the bazaar, the crowd increases. Amid this bustle it is difficult to imagine an account of the 1857 revolt by a local resident Zahir Dehlavi who described a late evening scene in Urdu Bazaar: '… it was completely quiet, and there was not a single bird to be heard or seen. Indeed, there was a strange silence over the whole town, as if the city had turned suddenly into a wilderness. Shops were lying looted, the doors of all the houses and havelis were closed, and there was not a glimmer of light.'

Wind up your walk at Matia Mahal chowk, soaking in the scenes, smells and sounds. There are tables laid on the side of the road, on which people are having chai, or munching on kebabs and egg parathas. The alley to the right goes to Gali Chooriwallan. Straight ahead is Chitli Qabar chowk, which has a florist shop (below) at the centre. If you take the left lane from there and keep straight, then left, then right, you emerge into Netaji Subhash Marg in Daryaganj. This is the Delhi we know. What we saw some time ago, however, lingers on like a dream.

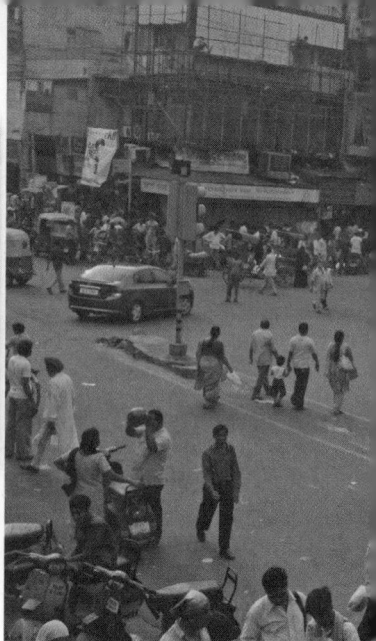

Chandni Chowk
Worlds within worlds

Open Mon-Sat (closed Sun)

It is exhilarating to sweep your eyes across the 360-degree view of this 'secular India' theme park dotted with temples, mosques, churches and gurdwaras. Masked Jains, kirpan-wielding Sikhs, saffron-robed sadhus and bearded mullahs carry on their daily spiritual pursuits. Sari-clad and burqa-clad women walk alongside immigrant labourers and foreign tourists. It is also amusing to spot the occasional 'first-world' New Delhiites making the excursion armed with mineral water bottles, hand sanitizer and shades. But the most pleasant thing in Chandni Chowk is to smell that pungent mix of sewage, sweat, dung, jalebis, bhallas and marigolds.

Begin your walk at the red **Digambar Jain Mandir**, famous for its bird hospital. A bhikshu sleeps under the heritage building status slab, while Western backpackers click pictures. They give way, just in time, to let the green Chandni Chowk shuttle bus rumble by. It is choked with local residents going to Ballimaran, Nai Sadak and Fatehpuri.

Just then appears a red-capped ear cleaner who offers to dewax the ears of a tourist. To break the language barrier, he takes out a needle, inserts it into his right ear and brings it out from his right nostril. Amid this chaos, it is easy to miss two stately sights—the

Baptist Church and the **State Bank of India**. And don't miss out on the **Seesganj Gurdwara**.

Chandni Chowk is a gastronomic delight and is lined with vendors selling chaat, fruits, desserts and ice creams. **Old Famous Jalebiwalla** is just a few steps away from the gurdwara, and the entry to parathewaali galli is close-by, while **Haldiram** is across the road. If you don't want to eat, keep walking, past stores selling Chinese toys, bras, saris, goggles, belts, burqas, chappals, until you reach a traffic light. The **Town Hall** on the right,

flecked with pigeons, looks straight out of London. Not surprising, since it was built a few years after the 1857 revolt. For that Piccadilly Circus touch, there are benches and lampposts. Crumbling havelis with claustrophobic histories line Chandni Chowk. The most famous and well preserved is **Lala Chunnamal ki Haveli**, where you can ask the owners for a quick look. Wind up your walk with a look at **Fatehpuri Masjid**, built in 1650 by a begum of Shah Jahan, and finally stop at the **Amritsari Lassiwalla** for cool and refreshing drink.

45

stroll

National Science Centre
New worlds

Where Near Gate No 1, Pragati Maidan
Open 10am-5:30pm (7 days) **Ticket** Rs 20 (under 5s free), 3D film Rs 10

Play

National Science Centre

Delhi Zoo

Dolls Museum

National Rail Museum

Adventure Island

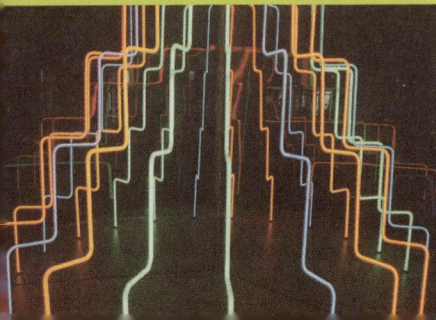

A ball floating in air with no regard for gravity; a seat of nails actually comfortable to sit on. Discovering science at the National Science Centre is fun. The learning is incidental and the exploration unending. Staircases lead up to more exhibition halls.

Galleries open up more wonders—including a cave

alive with the farting sound of dinosaurs—and an entire section devoted to replicas of these prehistoric giants. Thankfully there is no smell.

Beware of the maze of mirrors. You may get lost in their reflections. Get inside a giant kaleidoscope to see multiple reflections of yourself. Walk into a cabin to freeze your shadow. Those tormented by their big bully of a brother can extract revenge by having his head served on a breakfast tray – in real time. Make sure you attend the two 3-D shows that have horses, snakes and flying carpets ramming straight into the viewers.

If this is science, why do we hate it at school?

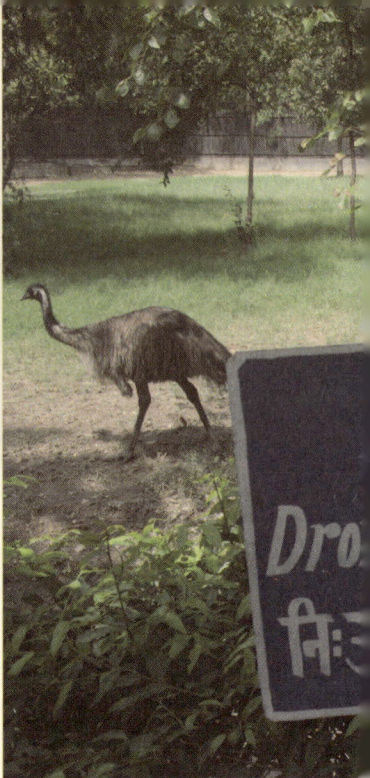

Perhaps the greatest charm of this zoological garden is its location, bordering the Purana Qila and overlooking its ramparts and leafy foliage. The zoo houses over 1,000 birds, mammals and reptiles; and an added attraction is the migratory birds that arrive in the winters, especially the painted storks and ducks.

As you buy a ticket and walk down the wide steps, a sense of anticipation builds up with the roar of the tigers carried through the air.

The reptile house is on the right – but you may leave it for the last, since more exciting animals and birds await.

The neatly gravelled pathways and aesthetic signage on stone slabs all add to the impression that this is the country's premier zoo.

Among the enclosures that

48

EMU

s novaehollandiae

Hab. AUSTRALLIA

are particularly exciting for children, is the leopard cage with numerous cats of varying sizes draped over the branches of trees, or sparring playfully with each other. The open tiger enclosure, with a moat, and similar spaces for rhinos, lions and crocodiles, offer many a thrilling moment for young wildlife enthusiasts.

A walk to the gharial pond, where the fish-eating reptiles lie in a lazy stupor, is recommended.

Other animals include sloth bears, a variety of deer and antelope, monkeys, chimpanzees and apes, giraffes, zebras, hippos, colourful African parrots and Australian cockatoos, emus and ostrich, among others. Pack a picnic lunch, but definitely don't share it with the animals—it's one of the most rash things to do, and is strictly prohibited.

play

Dolls Museum
The world of little folk

Where Nehru House, 4 Bahadur Shah Zafar Marg **Ticket** Adults Rs 15, children Rs 5 **Open** 10am-6pm (closed Mon)

Set up by the late cartoonist, K. Shankar Pillai, the Shankar International Dolls Museum has one of the largest collections of dolls (over 60,000) anywhere in the world.

Black, white, and brown; Bulgarian, Cuban, and Indian, walk past more than 160 glass cases and feel like Gulliver who is washed ashore during a shipwreck and awakens in a land with people a fraction of his size.

Meet the Kabuki dancer of Japan, Flamenco dancer of Spain, and the Jazz trumpeter of US. Watch the Siberian hunter travelling on a sledge, the Norwegian witch riding a broom, and a Portuguese girl carrying a chicken on her head. Say hello to baby Mozart and wave at the little astronaut.

There is even a doll-making workshop (left) at the museum. For everyone who is a child at heart, this is a world tour you will remember forever.

play

The Museum Junction at the National Rail Museum is probably the safest train station in Delhi. No child-lifting gangs operate here, coaches don't overturn, steam engines don't hiss, signals don't change colour and the tracks are padded with overgrown grass. But don't panic if your kids are not in sight and you hear real trains whistling by—a busy railway track lies outside the boundary.

Kids can easily clamber aboard the 1910 steam locomotive at the entrance. Inside, are more engines and locomotives of different periods. Peek inside the locked wagon that belonged to the Maharaja of Gaekwad. Parents will certainly be impressed

by the gold-enamelled ornate ceiling.

Be prepared for some real travel too. The Joy Express, with its box wagons and baby benches, chugs around every few minutes. It takes you on a chug-chug journey around the entire museum. A steam engine ride is a special treat reserved for Sundays. Check out the museum gallery. A glass case displays the skull of a wild elephant killed more than a century ago in a train collision. The train models are riveting. Push the button on a model steam engine to see fire glowing in the coal chamber. Another starts moving its axle with great sound and fury. And remember, there is no train home.

play

Adventure Island
Wheeeeee!

Where Sector 10, Rohini
Metro stop Rithala
Tickets Children + adults respectively: Weekdays Rs 220 + Rs 270, weekends + holidays Rs 270 + Rs 350

A mother shouts 'behave yourself' to her excited young charges as they soar 30 feet into the air on a ride called Z-force. The world stops for a fraction of a second. Whoosh. A free fall; mum screams the loudest. Dignity is compromised at the Adventure Island. People with the stiffest upper lips lose their inhibitions once they fasten their seatbelts on the Sidewinder.

Set around an artificial lake, Adventure Islnd has 14 rides in all. A bridge, resembling San Francisco's Golden Gate, separates the island from the mall, Metro Walk. Kids with mums, dads, bhaiyyas, didis, ammajis, baujis and buas walk past Costa Coffee and Benetton outlets to reach the scene of action. Tickets in hand, they are ready for thrills and chills.

The world-class rides have been sourced from firms that supply equipment to Disneyland.

Most are a mix of fun and fury. Beware of Twister. While lifting up the seated people in a gentle revolving movement, it abruptly turns upside down. Sandals drop, mobile phones fall, and it rains coins. Before the joy riders can recover, the axle furiously swirls 360 degrees. Rotating and revolving, tumbling and toppling, pitting levity against gravity, people seem fated to fall like flakes of tobacco from a broken cigar. But they don't.

The adventure ends, and your pulse rate comes back to normal, only to start racing again at the next ride.

There are other rides to explore—toy trains, airplanes, bumping cars, and sky riders. Parents don't be anxious. The safety measures are rigorous and the staff is alert and smart. They move around with a dustpan, just in case somebody throws up, and that's the only adventure to avoid.

Eat

Café Turtle

Indian Coffee House

Big Chill

Everest Café

Route 04 and 4S

Coffee Chains

With contributions
by Auroni Mookerjee

Café Turtle
Tasteful tranquillity

Where Khan Market;
N Block Market, GK I;
8 Nizamuddin East Market
Open 9.30am-9.30pm

Soft jazz, hand-painted thangkas, and hushed conversations. Every city needs a bubble where you can be who you want to be. Café Turtle is one such place. The book lovers read. The writers write. The fashionable display their Cartiers and Armanis.

Home to Delhi's 'refined' crowd, Café Turtle is the coffee shop above the iconic bookstore, Full Circle, at Khan Market. There is a clone, bookshop with café above, at GK I's N block market, and another in Nizamuddin East.

It may not serve the best food in town: its salads, sandwiches, cakes and pizzas are almost bland for Indian tastes, and it does not offer any non-vegetarian options. But the point of this café is not its cakes

and coffees. It is something to do with its character, which is intensely addictive.

The lighting is soft. The décor is not loud. The stewards are not intrusive. There are shelves stacked with spiritual books. Black and white photographs of Jazz artistes adorn the walls.

Each table has a bottle in the centre, with tender green stems of money plant sending roots out into the water. The entire effect is so soothing that the most noisy Delhiites lose their natural brashness and start speaking in hushed undertones as soon as they settle down. The clinking of forks and knives adds to the harmony. In winter, lounging in the al fresco area makes your mood sunnier and your fingers less icy.

But the Café Turtle experience is incomplete without exploring its sister concern, the bookstore below. To browse the shelves for an hour, to buy a novel and then walk up the wooden stairs and settle down to read—with something as simple as pita bread and hummus—is an experience almost bordering Proustian tranquillity. You feel lovely, fulfilled and rich.

eat

Indian Coffee House
Brewing up memories

Where Mohan Singh Place, Baba Kharak Singh Marg, Connaught Place
Open 9am-9pm

All revolutions emerge from coffee houses, which face an existential crisis when the masses get an appetite for bourgeois burgers. The Indian Coffee House is a classic example. In the rundown Mohan Singh Place shopping complex in Connaught Place, it was once the thinking person's getaway. Run by the Indian Coffee Workers' Cooperative Society, it is today a nostalgic place frequented only by those who wish to defy the diktats of coffee chains.

On breezy summer evenings, it is refreshing to sit outside on the terrace and look down at the fast-paced life of Connaught Place (a multiplex chain is a jump away). Alternatively, you can turn your back on that world and focus on your cutlet, coffee and Camus.

Inside, it is as if the world stopped half a century ago. The rotating blades of the ceiling fans languidly stir up the room's warm air, providing relief from the heat in the old-fashioned way. The sofas, it

58

must be confessed, are torn in places, but are very inviting. Ask the regulars why they come here and they will be unable to reply. That is why you need to hang out here. The Indian Coffee House, circa 1957, has a character that is addictive.

Earlier this café was situated where Palika Bazaar is now. It then moved to Janpath and finally to its present site in 1975. That year, the news of Indira Gandhi's Emergency first broke here, before the official announcement. In those days, the coffee house was a lively venue for writers, painters, musicians, philosophers and politicians. They seem to have moved to newer places, but some bits of the past have survived.

Stewards still wear a uniform, tea is still served from a teapot, and the quality of the masala dosa is superior. And no one raises an eyebrow if you bury your nose in your book. Here you can experience what the capital once was, and is losing out now in the race to become a bustling megacity.

eat

Blueberry cheesecake. There's a reason it became a south Delhi phenomenon. It has caused a lot of people from all walks of life to melt. Bulky men, squabbling women, crying babies, pregnant moms, growling dads, it has worked wonders for all. And the only place to get it in Delhi is Big Chill.

What started out as a cute little café in Kailash Colony, serving hand-cranked ice creams, frozen yogurts and a selection of Italian dishes, has slowly morphed into an iconic restaurant with larger premises at Khan Market.

Sure it doesn't have the same quaint charm of the past, but today's lively bustle and buzz more than makes up for it. It is a bit painful to try and get a table at any of the branches and prices have gone up over time, but it's worth the hassle. Your poison of choice ranges from sugar, cream, chocolate, to oodles of melting cheese.

The menu is so extensive (however, mainly within the family of confectionaries, frozen desserts and Italian cuisine) that you can go back every week for an entire year, and still not have sampled everything. And if Big Chill has one thing going for itself, it's the feel-good punch that comes with every milk shake, baked potato, pasta, pizza and cheesecake. It's perfect for any occasion—lunches, dates, birthdays, random celebrations, cravings or just sheer gluttony.

Everest Café

Nepal recreated

Where H No 4591, Dal Mandi, near Hotel Star Palace, Paharganj
Open 7am-11pm

Tucked away in a shaded lane off the main street of Paharganj, Everest Café is total hippy—it looks shabby, feels cool. Wicker chairs and low tables occupy a space so small that you sometimes find yourself squeezing against dozens of visiting backpackers. But no matter how cramped the café is, the dim lamps make you relaxed and happy. Even stray dogs come in here to take a nap. The place has mood.

It is popular among Delhi's foreign budget tourists, and different languages and accents twitter, turning it into an informal UN canteen.

Since the owner is Nepali, the music is usually Nepali songs of love and longing. Framed on the wall, there is a Kathmandu newspaper with headlines of the 2001 royal family massacre.

No wonder then that there's a Nepali thali (as well as yak cheese) on the menu. But if you visit on a hot summer day, order the green salad. Spread on a bed of moist lettuce leaves, fresh vegetables come tossed with sesame seeds in a yogurt dressing (mayonnaise on request). For the main course, ask for lemon-grilled chicken, which strikes a fine balance with mashed potato and steamed vegetables.

Do not miss the vegetable momos. These steamed dumplings are delicate, and complemented by the sauce, which is sesame-flavoured rather than the usual red chilli paste. For dessert, try the chocolate cake. It is a crumbly slice with a crusty top. Finally, wash the meal down with ginger-honey tea.

If you like to read with your meals, *Lonely Planet* guides are stacked in one corner. You may also spot classics such as *War and Peace* and *David Copperfield*. One of the chapters in Sam Miller's *Delhi: Adventures in a Megacity* opens in the Everest Café.

eat

These two restaurants are combined in one write-up because they are among the most popular watering holes for young people. They are centrally located, play good music, show exciting sporting events and, most importantly, are easy on the pocket. With close to endless happy hours, you can see why every college kid and young adult in the city considers these places their second home. Yet in concept, the two are worlds apart.

At Route 04 (pictured) you'll never find an empty table. Nestled within the Khan Market middle lane, in theme and décor it's a far more affordable TGIF. It's far more popular among those born in the '90s. Besides the cheap booze, an entire floor dedicated to smokers and loud rock & roll seals the deal for most of the regulars.

4S started off as any run-of-the-mill Punjabi Chinese joint in Defence Colony market. Add to that happy hours, and it suddenly became one of the most popular hangouts for college students.

It does have a far more old school family restaurant and bar feel to it, and hence is more popular among the '80s generation. But that's what makes it great, that same old feeling, like nothing will ever change in this space. Same smiling waiters, moustached doorman, peppery chicken, crispy lamb, Old Monk and Coke—it's a place which never fails to take you back.

Route 04 and 4S
Young at heart

Route 04 Khan Market
Hours 10am-12.30am
4S Defence Colony Market
Open Noon-midnight

eat

Coffee Chains
When chai isn't enough

It's a funny thing. In this city you are likely to find a hot cup of tea every 50 metres. It'll be hot, milky and ridiculously cheap. Each one of these joints will have a friendly-looking proprietor. Sounds charming, right?

Well, as it turns out, not charming enough for some Delhiites. Instead they are turning to mass-designed orange, purple, red and other hideously coloured coffee bars, situated in the foyer of every mall and office building, or eating up every departmental store you knew so well in your neighbourhood market. To get to a lot of them you need to pay parking, which may cost more or as much as your cuppa.

Of course coffee, not chai is the preferred beverage at these places. Not biskut but biscotti is what you nibble on.

But it's true, the city loves every Barista, Café Coffee Day, Costa Coffee and other such chains, franchising the hell out of real estate. The crowd that can afford to spend about Rs 100 per cup of brew, with double the amount thrown in for mass-produced snacks, has made these joints their regular hangout. After all, as one coffee chain says in its advertising, 'A lot can happen over coffee'.

Mercifully, these coffee bars serve genuinely brewed coffee, and not the instant stuff. You can choose to add your diet sweetener or brown sugar. The staff is smiling and educated and sucker you into adding chocolate sauce and whipped cream in everything. And the cherry on the top: they have air-conditioning.

It's convenient for get-togethers, meetings and, yes, even dates (they're casual after all). It's funny how convenience just puts a whole new spin on, well, fast food coffee. You've got to be lovin' it.

eat

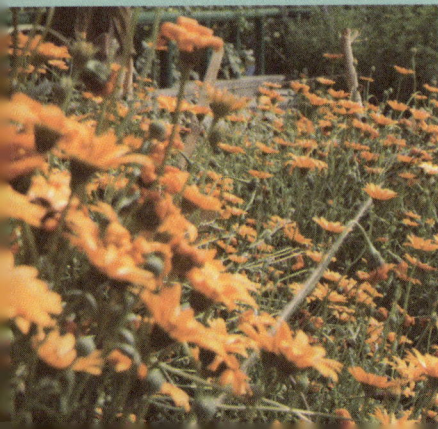

Delhi offers plenty by the way of refuge in its public parks. Scattered all over the city, some of them stand out as green havens where one can escape for a moment from the insistent pace of city life.

Central Park in Connaught Place has the busy Rajiv Chowk metro terminus rumbling beneath it, but the garden itself is an urban grove of clipped hedges, cascading fountains, gentle slopes and an amphitheatre. In the evenings, tired office workers lie down on the grass, children run around, lovers get closer, and solitary souls read novels; and in case anyone misses civilization, the showrooms dazzle just across the road.

The **Lodhi Garden**, a landscaped emerald patch set around historic tombs, is a favourite haunt of anyone wanting to savour a breath of fresh air in the middle of the city. Its scenic track is crowded with joggers and walkers, morning and evening. You can catch up on your exercise, do a spot of birding, explore medieval heritage, as well as learn to identify trees and plants in this multi-faceted oasis.

Breathe

Delhi Parks

Hailey Road

Gandhi–King Plaza

Tonga Rides

Delhi Parks
Leafy retreats

breathe

The **Deer Park** at Hauz Khas is a gem in South Delhi. You can go for walks and picnics, enjoy the company of deer, rabbits and peacocks, and then head to the monument complex.

Favoured by ministers, bureaucrats and expats, **Nehru Park** (Chanakyapuri) is as pruned and civilized as its immediate neighbourhood. It is also occasionally the venue of memorable musical soirees.

Buddha Jayanti Park at Dhaula Kuan is favoured by romantic couples who get cosy under the watchful eyes of a Buddha statue. Nobody bothers them except the occasional eunuchs selling blessings.

The neatly-landscaped **Indraprastha Park** on Ring Road is 2.7 km long and boasts a white pagoda. It has pretty features like the Smriti Van

and a fragrant garden planted with flowers.

Gardens have their special charm, but the most favoured open expanse among Delhiites is the sprawling grounds of **India Gate**. People from different walks of life, in this class-driven city, converge at the 'maidan' with friends, lovers and families and forget their differences for a while. The rich, poor, powerful and powerless gather to buy balloons, have ice creams or take photographs.

One of Delhi's most unlikely green escapes is the park at Rajiv Gandhi Sethu, better known as the **AIIMS flyover**. By 9 pm the evening rush hour thins to a trickle, the smog disappears and the temperature drops. The water sprinklers keep the grass wet and the air fragrant with the scent of damp earth.

The gardens have outlandish 'steel sprouts' installations, which the children love to climb. The grown ups prefer lounging on the slopes. Till late at night, women play kabaddi, men play cards and teens play badminton and cricket. Despite being in the city's heart, it seems far removed from the urban chaos.

breathe

The regular guided walks in Delhi (think Chandni Chowk) are intense, but they ignore the languid charm of the city. Tucked behind the high rises of Connaught Place, Hailey Road is a traffic-free stretch with tree-lined pavements, old-world bungalows, mossy brick walls and a 14th-century ruin. A leisurely stroll here shows off Delhi at its serene best.

Start your walk at about 8.30am from the Iranian Embassy on Barakhamba Road. Rather than walking on the left, cross over to the other side. It is richer in sounds and sights. Soon you will reach Asha Deep, an apartment complex of 44 flats. It is fronted by a handsome palm tree, which if seen from an angle, appears taller than the building itself. The bungalow next to it, however, merits more detailed attention even though you can't enter it. The gates of No 7 are locked and its driveway has disappeared under a soft bed of wild grass. The abandoned brick mansion inside transports you to Manderley of Daphne du Maurier's *Rebecca*.

Next door (No 8) used to be the legendary Montessori school founded by 'Aunty Gauba' where generations of toddlers were nurtured through their

Hailey Road
Ambling adventure

Where Opp Modern School, Barakhamba Rd
Best time Winter (any time), summer (early mornings and evenings)

alphabets and nursery rhymes. Nearby is a chai booth popular with auto drivers. You may like to sit down on the low platform, below the giant peepal tree, to have a chai and samosas, served with chhola, for breakfast.

Now, walk straight ahead. You will head for Banga Bhawan–whose only interesting feature is its VIP entry (typically Delhi). Ignore it, and walk towards a right turn. On turning,

you will see the 14th-century Maharaja Agrasen Baoli, an ancient step-well. This amazing ruin is always deserted, and you can explore it at leisure. On walking further down the lane, you will find that both sides of the street are lined with clothes hung out to dry.

Next to the Shiva temple is a dhobi ghat where you will see dozens of dhobis washings mounds of clothes in tubs, a rare sight in this age of washing machines.

Continue with your walk along the forlorn low brick wall. A few more steps and this alley will join Hailey Lane. Turn left and enter a leafy haven of dense trees—nature finds it own way, even in the heart of a concrete metropolis. A minute's stroll and you emerge into the busy Tolstoy Marg.

Your journey ends.

breathe

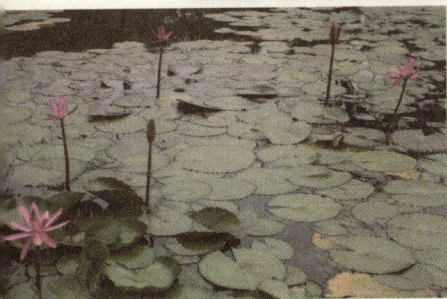

Gandhi-King Plaza
Macondo of the mind

Where India International Centre (IIC), 40 Max Mueller Marg

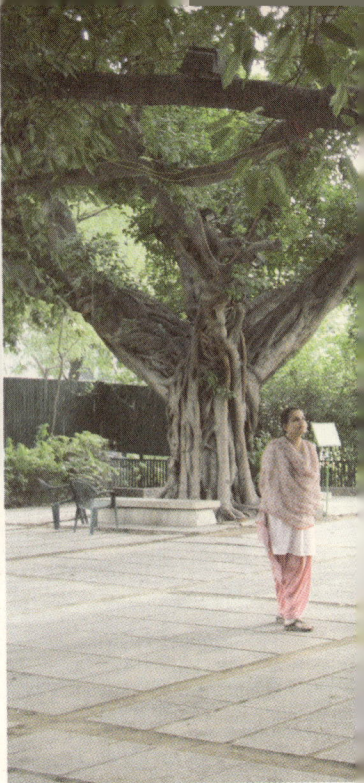

This is a snug little pool garden at one corner of the India International Centre (IIC), Delhi's so-called intellectual hub, which hosts exhibitions, music and dance concerts, and book readings almost every week. As you enter the IIC gate, rather than going straight to the foyer, turn left from the driveway, to a pavement lined with potted plants. A few steps straight ahead, then up a few stairs, through a low gate, and you are inside one of the city's best-kept secrets.

The IIC, designed by American architect Joseph Allen Stein, was opened in 1962, and the plaza is as old. The first thing you see is a brick pillar with the sayings of Mahatma Gandhi and Martin Luther King on all four sides (hence the name). But the truly incredible sight is that of two enormous fig trees, giving the plaza a permanent shade. They are like characters out of

some magic-realism novel, their trunks wrapped in a union of graceful folds. The cover photo of Arundhati Roy's novel *The God of Small Things* was shot at the lovely pool here. It has that same dark green water, those same floating leaves, and the same pink water lilies.

While the ground stays cool under the shade of trees, there is a little sunny patch towards one end, which becomes the most precious space in winter.

Every element here conspires to lull you into tranquillity, be it the two giant trees, the cane chairs, the stony landscape, and the chatter of the birds, or the pool.

They all intermingle to create a Macondo of the mind, a place with no contact with the outside world. When you want to reconnect with the universe, just walk a few yards to the IIC building and step into a concert at the auditorium.

breathe

E very year the newspapers report that the authorities are planning to banish the tongas of Old Delhi to address the city's traffic problem. Sentimental pieces appear in their defence and every year, somehow, they manage to survive.

Not a popular commuting option any longer, they are found in old neighbourhoods such as Kashmiri Gate, Sadar Bazaar and Daryaganj. Evenings and night are the best time for a joy ride. Like in the magical world of Harry Potter, the tonga trots on giving an illusion of poles, trees and houses hopping aside to clear the way for the moody mare to chart her own course. It jolts the passengers, splashes over puddles, overtakes buses,

Tonga Rides
Journeys recalled

Where In front of Delhi railway station or under the bridge near New Delhi railway station (Paharganj side)
Cost Rs 50 (negotiable)
Best time Early evening

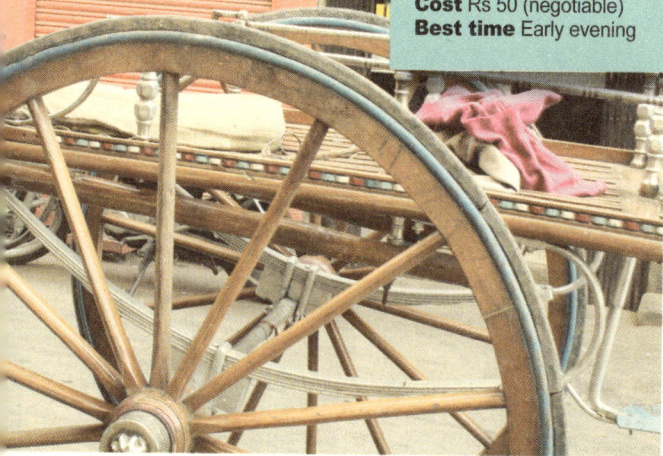

gets honked at by SUVs and jumps the traffic lights.

You pass by the city's rundown landmarks, the wind ruffles through your hair and a strange light-headed feeling takes you by surprise. At the final destination, the tonga stops, the mare relaxes, the tongawalla has a smoke and the return journey begins, rushing past streets lined with crumbling mansions and ancient trees.

During the entire ride, the constant clip-clop of the mare's hooves maintains a regular beat against the rumble of trains, honking of cars and whoosh of the metro. A forgotten world of black-and-white movies and romantic melodies is brought alive.

breathe

National Museum
Historic treasures

Where Janpath **Open**
10am-5pm (closed Mon)
Tickets Indians Rs 10,
students Re 1, others Rs 300
(inclusive of audio tour)

Muse

National Museum

NGMA

Mandi House Area

Timeless Art Book Studio

India Habitat Centre

The past gets tangible here. With over 200,000 exhibits, spanning more than 5,000 years, the National Museum, India's largest, is a storehouse of heritage. It has three floors. Its corridors are lined with 800 sculptures, from the 3rd century BC to the 18th century AD. The exhibition halls have statues, paintings and knick-knacks such as coins, toys and pottery.

There is also a woman's skeleton, with pottery shards arranged around her head, indicating that people of the Harappan civilization believed in life after death.

With each gallery dedicated to a theme or period (Harappan civilization, Maurya dynasty, Sunga and Satvahana art, Gandhara sculptures), it is unsettling to walk through so many centuries in so little time.

And almost each item, no matter if it's just a terracotta animal, can be observed and admired for hours.

The Gandhara sculpture is remarkable for its Greek influence; some of its Buddhas are dressed in togas. The gallery on Buddhism has thangkas, or painted scrolls from Tibet, wooden sculptures from Java and Cambodia, and Buddha's life scenes from Sarnath.

It is most renowned for its Buddha relics (5th to 4th century BC) unearthed from Piprahwa in the Bastar district.

The section on Indian miniature paintings, with more than 300 exhibits, could well make for a separate museum. Belonging chiefly to Mughal, Rajasthani and Pahari styles, most paintings, dating from 1000 to 1900, are inspired from scenes out of Hindu epics, court life and classical dance and music. A few show the remarkably liberal lifestyle of the era: embracing lovers, bathing women and harem princesses enjoying wine and music.

Other floors display textiles, musical instruments, coins and weapons.

An exhibit that must not be missed is outside the building. The octagonal chariot (18th to 19th century) from Tamil Nadu, near the entrance gate, is made of saal and sagvan wood. Dedicated to Vishnu, it has six wheels, 425 carved panels and weighs more than 2,000 kg. It will take your breath away.

muse

Set up in 1954 at Jaipur House near India Gate, the National Gallery of Modern Art's old wing, has stately marble flooring and arched corridors.

One of the wing's two sections devotes itself to the works of Indian painters; the other is a permanent gallery of paintings by international artists. Chilean artist Arturo Pacheco Altamiran's *Ships at Anchor* resonates with personal journeys yet to be undertaken. Bosnian artist Mersard Berber's *Chronicle of Sarajevo* with its neighing horses and a melancholic pasha hints at the dark Balkan history. *The Holy Cow* by a Japanese painter makes Indians look exotic in their own eyes.

The new wing (2009) comprising five floors over two blocks takes the visitor into a journey of modern Indian art, from the 19th century to the present. The basement level shows Indian miniatures and European artwork.

The next level displays 19th-century India as an oriental fantasy. The sharp-lined temples, mosques, devdasis (temple goddesses), brides, kotwals (constables), sweepers, warriors were painted by Indians for their British masters.

muse

Called 'Company painting', this art married the miniature tradition of Rajput and Mughal painting with the Western perspective. Raja Ravi Varma's masterpieces in oil, the pinnacle of this Indo-Western style, are on this floor.

The third level pulsates with sensuous energy. The works of Amrita Shergil, the Lahore-based painter who died young, is a principal attraction. The naked brown girl, the woman with sagging breasts, the two European women, a group of Brahmin boys...Shergil's people throb with emotional vitality. Her self-portrait is the most flamboyant: the shoulders bare, the hair loose, and the smile showing bliss. Even her *Still Life*, with its three eggs and a water jug, has passion.

On the fourth level, some of India's contemporary masters, also the most expensive, are exhibited: Satish Gujral, Tyeb Mehta, F.N. Souza, S.H. Raza and M.F. Husain.

On the first floor of the second block (new wing), the giant *Connaught Place* by Jaswant Singh cannot be missed. It shows a man with one eye and no face. Behind him are the corridors and pillars of Delhi's erstwhile British commercial centre, which gives its name to the painting.

On the second level of this block, there are photographs by Raghu Rai, Dayanita Singh and Ketaki Seth, and paintings of film stars like Madhubala and Nargis Dutt. Those familiar with Bollywood will feel at home here.

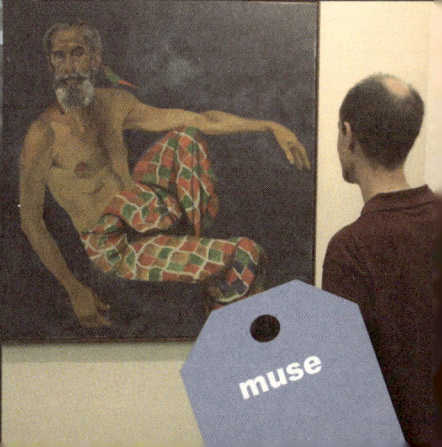

muse

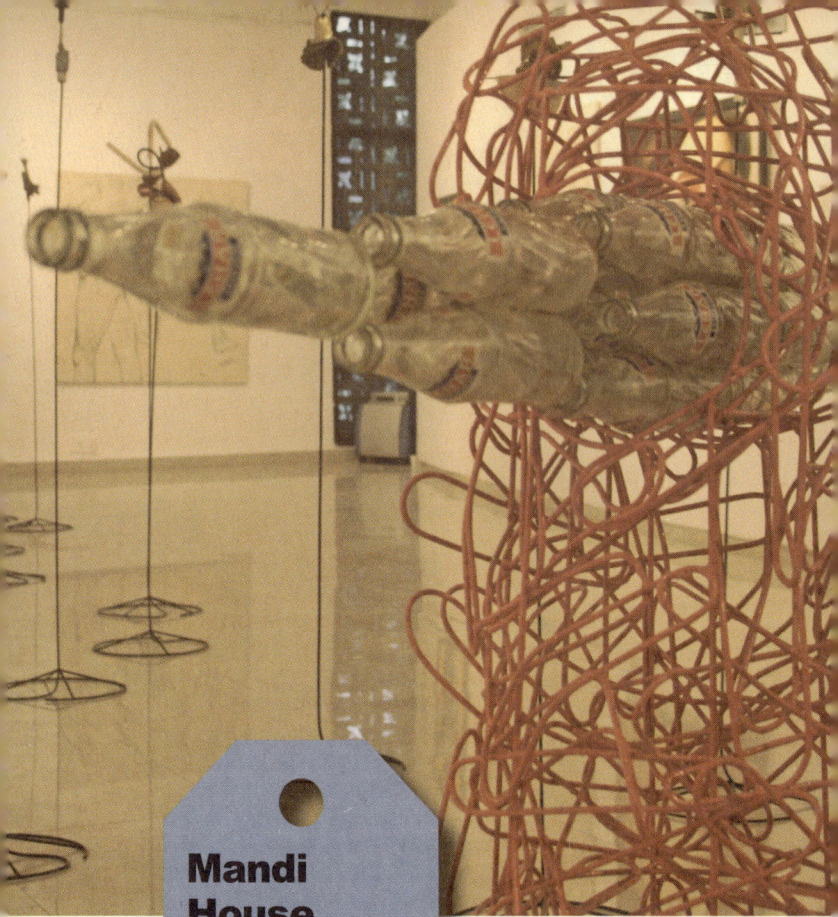

Mandi House Area
Inspiring art spaces

Where Near CP
Metro Stop Mandi House

Actors are rehearsing on the lawn of the Mandi House traffic roundabout. A book reading is on at the Triveni garden theatre, while people browse at the art exhibitions inside. A musical is being performed at Kamani Auditorium. A theatre festival

busy circle has Russian poet Alexander Pushkin's statue (overleaf) at one corner, one of its avenues is named after Tansen, India's greatest classical musician, and another is named after Safdar Hashmi, a modern playwright.

Triveni Kala Sangam has four art galleries, a bookshop, an auditorium, a serene garden and a lovely canteen. A city institution, Triveni offers classes in painting, photography and sculpture. Its art galleries— Art Heritage, Shridharani Gallery, Sculpture Court and Triveni Gallery (left)—are among Delhi's most coveted venues to exhibit paintings and photographs. The garden theatre is popular for book events and drama and poetry readings. The open-air terrace canteen, offering a lovely view of the theatre, is a crowd puller during lunch hour. The simple home-style shami kebabs and carrot cakes are better than what your mother makes.

is being inaugurated in the National School of Drama.

Mandi House area near Connaught Place, which gets its name from the imposing Doordarshan headquarters situated there, is the hub of some of the most premier cultural spaces in Delhi. Its

From Bharat Natyam performances, to Krishna Lila and Shakespearean comedies, the **Kamani Auditorium** hosts them all. With a seating capacity of 632, the auditorium has had some of the world's best actors performing here.

Adjoining Kamani is the **Shriram Bharatiya Kala Kendra**, another important cultural space.

The **National School of Drama** (NSD) is India's most prestigious theatre-training institute. Just strolling in the compound is like hiding in a green room and eavesdropping on actors' conversations as they prepare for a play.

At the surrounding chai stalls, you hear the NSD students talking passionately about acting techniques, playwrights and directors. It's not a bad idea to make friends. Some of India's best-known Bollywood actors are NSD graduates and, who knows, you may bond with a star of tomorrow? Every year in January, NSD organizes Bharat Rang Mahotsav, a

theatre festival that pulls in talent from across the country. It has a special place in Delhi's cultural calendar.

Other cultural spaces in Mandi House are Rabindra Bhawan, the Shri Ram Centre for Performing Arts, FICCI Auditorium, Lalit Kala Academy, Sahitya Kala Academy, Sapru House Library, Sangeet Natak Academy, and Meghdoot Theatre Complex. Check newspaper listings for their events. If art gets too intense, relief can be found by walking up Tansen Marg to the nearby Bengali Market. The two famous fast food joints —Bengali Sweet House and Nathu's—are wildly popular for their chaat and desserts. For coffee drinkers, there is a Costa Coffee outlet.

Timeless Art Book Studio

Lost in bookland

Where South Extension I
Open 7 days, 10am-8pm

It has some of the most expensive coffee table books under one roof in Delhi. Spread across 1,600 sq ft, Timeless Art Book Studio is a rich world of Italian marbles, teak furniture and a louvred French window. The most expensive book here, *The Godfather Family Album*, costs Rs 40,000.

But this is not just any coffee table bookstore. There is a plasma screen television, love seats, lecterns, footrests, rocking chairs, a six-seater dining table and ... hold your pajamas ... a double bed! There is also an Enfield bike in the centre of the studio.

The owner, the South Asia distributor of well-known art book houses, designed this place as a 'personal library'. One can spend an entire day sprawled on the bed flipping through wrist-breaking tomes on the Himalayas, Rajasthani palaces, Hollywood legends and world architecture. And of course, the collection of art books is extensive, covering Indian and international artists. Patronized by designers, architects, artists, collectors, actors, authors, and foreign diplomats, the studio stands on the boundary of the dusty Kotla village. Its interior is so different from the world outside, that when you emerge after spending a day here, you almost start believing that art cannot imitate real life.

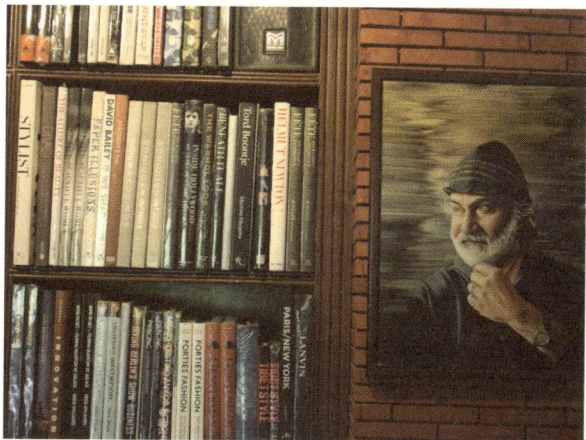

India
Habitat
Centre
Culture
hub

Where Lodhi Road

Joseph Allen Stein, the architect behind India Habitat Centre (IHC), who died before the opening of the complex, would have little imagined that this collection of six restaurants, four galleries, auditorium, amphitheatre and sprawling atrium would be so thoroughly exploited by the Delhi elite set who seek more than just Bollywood, cricket and shopping.

The Capital's cultural hub is known for hosting plays, book readings, music concerts, dance performances, film screenings, art exhibitions, corporate luncheons and office workshops. It is also a place to catch up with friends, family and colleagues.

Flowerpots line the steps to the foyer, a musical totem pole, at the entrance of Palm Court, tilts to produce melodious chimes. Inside, the vast skylight brightens the tree-decked courtyard. The roof's shading devices of blue-and-white panels screen off the sun's rays so that the area remains relatively cool even in summer.

Landscaped with abstract stone sculptures, the space is quiet, except for the sound of fountains or occasional laughter. Couples sit by the pools or on the plaza steps adjoining Stein auditorium.

On a rare day, you may run into college students rehearsing for their play in the amphitheatre. Art lovers wander around the galleries and culture enthusiasts hover outside the convention centre.

Hungry people feed on pizzas and chaat in the multi-cuisine Eatopia (bottom left), or on pancakes and hot dogs at The All American Diner (bottom right). The other restaurants, Delhi 'O' Delhi, Oriental Octopus and The Deck, are for members only. But no worries. The aesthetic spaces of IHC are accessible to all. Cultural programmes, exhibitions and discussions are attended avidly by all of Delhi's culture lovers.

Sufi Spaces
Oases of peace

There are not seven, but eight, cities in Delhi. The eighth is the most exciting. It has love, passion, music, poetry, tombs, domes and djinns. This city of Sufis is totally Islamic, but non-Muslims are welcome.

With no fixed geography, it is spread all over—from Mehrauli to Turkman Gate, from Kaka Nagar to Karkardooma Mor. It is identifiable by its dargahs, or shrines. They are everywhere, from near the crowded Jama Masjid, to outside the posh Oberoi hotel. Entire settlements have sprung up around some, while others lie ignored on roadsides.

In the pre-dawn hours, the dome at **Hazrat Nizamuddin Auliya** remains drowned in darkness, yet looks pleasant and

restful. Soon the muezzin will give a call, the beggars will wake up, the khadims (caretakers) will come in, the shrine's door will open and Delhi's 14th-century mystic will again cast the spell of his samaa (trance-like atmosphere).

This is Delhi's most touristy dargah. Any time is a good time to visit. The romantics find the air here to be saturated with sad, selfless love. The poet Amir Khusro and the princess Jahanara both loved Nizamuddin; both are buried close to him. Then there are the qawwals, whose forefathers have been singing here for the last 750 years. The qawwalis take place daily after the maghreeb (evening) prayers, with a special session on Thursday evenings (above).

A little distance down the road, in Kaka Nagar, is a dargah dedicated to a woman—**Bibi Fatima**. This is an unlikely setting for a shrine—no crowded alleys or kebab stalls around. Revamped a few years ago, the dargah now looks almost sterile. But appearances are deceptive. The caretaker warns of resident djinns.

Nearby, at the DDA park, Mathura Road, you have to climb a hillock to reach an open-air dargah, canopied by giant neem trees. There are three tombs, all covered with colourful chaadars.

The reigning 'baba', name unknown, is not as popular as Nizamuddin, but devotees do appear. Apart from prayers, they also fill the special water pots for birds.

95

If you are hungry, hop across the road to **Matka Pir**'s dargah (also famous for its biryani and kebab shop). Here, the tree branches are weighed down with clay pots that are the traditional thanksgiving to Shaikh Abu Bakr, aka Matka Baba. You may climb the stairs to the dargah, or first go to the adjacent stall to have kebabs with rumali rotis. Biryani, however, is sold only on advance order.

Khwaja Baqi Billah's shrine in the Sadar Bazaar graveyard is Delhi's quietest. This is a world away from the south Delhi dargahs. No qawwals, no khadims, no beggars. Only trees, tombs, dry leaves, occasional pilgrims and crows perched on tombstones. Connaught Place is 10 minutes away, but that seems unbelievable.

One of Delhi's oldest Sufi shrines is that of **Qutubuddin Bakhtiar Kaki**, (far right) in Mehrauli. Set in a courtyard, surrounded by unadorned tombs and meditative prayer halls, it is an ideal place to get away from the world and be with yourself.

explore

**Daryaganj
Book Bazaar
Buy the
book**

Where Netaji Subhash Rd
Open Sundays, 10am-6pm

There are two kinds of Delhiites—those who have been to the weekly book bazaar at Daryaganj and those who haven't. The former doesn't want the latter to know that each Sunday, the mile-long footpath between Delite cinema and the Daryaganj footbridge disappears under novels, memoirs, whodunits, quiz books, classics, encyclopedias, coffee table books, pulp fiction, foreign magazines and, sometimes, rare first editions.

Kuldeep Raj Nanda, whose stall is just below the iron pedestrian bridge, claims to be the first one to have set up a stall at Daryaganj. Over the decades, the little stretch of booksellers has extended from the bridge to Golcha Cinema, on to the telephone exchange near Dilli Gate, to Delite cinema. Besides second-hand books, stock is bought in containers from the United States and Canada to Bombay and Gujarat. Bulk dealers buy at the ports and then sell it to retailers such as these.

Next to Hotel Broadway, Surinder Dhawan's stall of about 3,000 books has everything, from J.K. Rowling, Jane Austen and Jackie Collins, to exotic cookbooks. While Dhawan has 20,000 books in his godown in Nihal Vihar, he displays just a fraction. But it's enough to attract booklovers from as far as Uttar Pradesh, Punjab, Chandigarh and Rajasthan.

The low pricing adds to the appeal. In a regular bookshop, you get Toni Morrison's *Beloved* for Rs 400, while Dhawan offers its first edition (hardbound!) for just Rs 100.

Look out for Muhammad Javed's stall opposite the telephone exchange, near the Shiva statue. His collection looks really second-hand: dog-eared pages, cracked spines, and scratched covers. Javed lives in south Delhi's Jamia Nagar and when people of Kalkaji, Sarita Vihar and Okhla want to dump their grandparents' books, they call him. That's why his collection is so eclectic. Gore Vidal's gay short stories, anecdotes of Prince Charles as a young bachelor, Shobha De's *Starry Nights*, or a handy hardbound *Jane Eyre*.

Literature is boring to many, but even they must read—if not Boris Pasternak, then Bill Gates. Mukesh Tiwari's stall, next to Javed's, is ideal for those who need cheap 'course books'. Here is a one-stop destination for books on computer programming, surgery and electrical engineering. IAS and MBA aspirants, too, will be breathless with excitement.

If your legs don't tire easily, the Sunday book bazaar has rare gems to offer. I once found a first edition of Ernest Hemingway's *The Old Man and the Sea* buried under a pile of John Grisham paperbacks—for Rs 100. Just scavenge, scavenge, scavenge.

explore

Before Delhi High Court legalized gay sex in 2009, the places for gay people to interact in the city were few. Besides parks for cruising and farmhouses for discreet parties, there was no watering hole except Pegs N Pints, the first nightclub in Delhi to offer a regular weekly night to gay people. The club's unofficial Tuesday 'gay night' was camouflaged as a 'private party', but it became wildly popular by word-of-mouth.

Every week, gay people would come to dance and to look for partners. Nothing has changed since then in the nightclub, except that it has lost its exclusivity.

After the landmark verdict, more pubs and clubs have started offering gay special nights, in order to grab their share of the pink paisa. Among these are Cibo in Hotel Janpath (Wednesdays or Saturdays); Ai in MGF Metropolitan Mall, Saket (not regularly); and Baci in Sundar Nagar (Tuesdays).

The premier cultural spaces, such as India Habitat Centre, regularly host gay-themed film festivals and book readings. In other words, gay people are becoming as boring as straight.

Gay Hangouts
Out and about

However, Pegs N Pints still retains the subversive feel of the old times on its Tuesday nights.

The crowd comes in after ten. Boys gyrate to chartbusters with teasing smiles and roving eyes. Lovers jiggle together, friends hug and single people sit alone stamping their feet to the music. By the next hour, the action also moves to the floor upstairs.

Boozing men huddle on sofas, some sit on the laps of others. As the clock ticks to 1am, the music becomes louder, Bollywood chartbusters are replayed, more vodka bottles are opened, kisses become desperate and embraces hungrier.

At 2am, the music stops and the lights come on. Life comes back to the straight world.

explore